THE PREDICTIONS LIBRARY

DREAMS

David V. Barrett

DORLING KINDERSLEY
London · New York · Stuttgart

A DORLING KINDERSLEY BOOK

Senior Editor • Sharon Lucas
Art Editor • Anna Benjamin
Managing Editor • Krystyna Mayer
Managing Art Editor • Derek Coombes
DTP Designer • Cressida Joyce
Picture Researcher • Becky Halls
Production Controller • Sarah Fuller
US Editor • Connie Mersel

First American Edition, 1995
2 4 6 8 10 9 7 5 3 1

Published in the United States by Dorling Kindersley Publishing, Inc.,
95 Madison Avenue, New York, New York 10016

Distributed by Houghton Mifflin Company, Boston.

Library of Congress Cataloging-in-Publication Data

Barrett, David V.
    Dreams / by David V. Barrett. -- 1st American ed.
        p.   cm. -- (The predictions library)
    ISBN 0-7894-0309-9
    1. Dreams. I. Title.   II. Series: Barrett, David V.   Predictions
library.
BF1078.B287   1995
135'.3 --dc20   95-11678
                                                                    CIP

Reproduced by Bright Arts, Hong Kong
Printed and bound in Hong Kong by Imago

CONTENTS

INTRODUCING
DREAMS

DREAMS HAVE BEEN A SOURCE OF FASCINATION FOR
CENTURIES – FROM THE ANCIENT BELIEF THAT DREAMS
FORETELL THE FUTURE TO THE MODERN APPROACH OF
LEARNING HOW TO INTERPRET YOUR DREAMS.

Everyone dreams during three or four periods of sleep every night. If we recall our dreams, they may seem to be a meaningless jumble of images, sometimes with a strong emotion attached, or with a coherent, though not always logical, storyline.

Some people believe that dreams are random thoughts around which our waking mind weaves a story, while others believe that our unconscious mind is telling itself stories. Dreams have also been considered to be messages from a spiritual source, memories of the past, or prophecies of the future.

The uncensored nature of dreams has troubled many thinkers, including Plato (c. 428–348 BC), who wrote

DEEP SLEEP
*This 18th-century personification
of sleep suggests how dreams open
the doorways of our minds,
enabling us to see inside ourselves.*

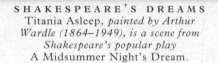

SHAKESPEARE'S DREAMS
Titania Asleep, *painted by Arthur Wardle (1864–1949), is a scene from Shakespeare's popular play* A Midsummer Night's Dream.

that "In all of us, even in good men, there is a lawless wild-beast nature, which peers out in sleep."

From the Dark Ages, hermits who had withdrawn from society to be closer to God seemed particularly troubled by erotic dreams. However, these dreams were often excused as being lewd temptations sent by the Devil to try to draw the hermit away from God. Another convenient excuse for these erotic dreams was the theory that every dream meant its exact opposite – therefore, even if a dream was sexual, it could still be enjoyed because it indicated inner purity and a healthy immortal soul.

BIBLICAL
DREAMS

THE BIBLE CONTAINS MANY EXAMPLES OF PEOPLE
WANTING TO KNOW WHAT THEIR DREAMS SIGNIFY. IT
LINKS DREAMS AND VISIONS WITH PROPHETS AND
MESSAGES FROM GOD.

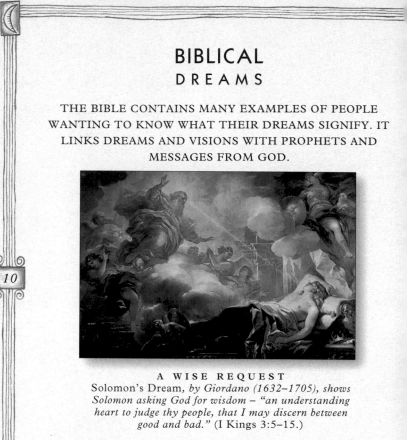

A WISE REQUEST
Solomon's Dream, *by Giordano (1632–1705), shows
Solomon asking God for wisdom – "an understanding
heart to judge thy people, that I may discern between
good and bad."* (I Kings 3:5–15.)

Probably the best-known
Biblical dream is the
Egyptian Pharaoh dreaming
of "seven well-favored kine
(cattle) and fat-fleshed,"
followed by seven more, "ill-
favored and lean-fleshed,"
which eat the first seven.
Pharaoh then dreams of
seven good ears of corn being
devoured by "seven thin ears
blasted with the east wind."

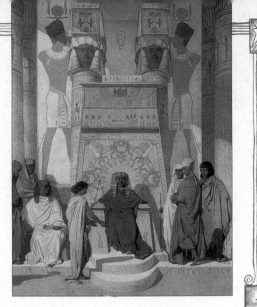

PHARAOH'S DREAMS
These dreams were prophetic, warning of a future calamity that could be avoided if the dreams were interpreted correctly and the interpretation acted upon. Joseph explaining Pharaoh's Dream *was painted by Jean Adrien Guignet (1816–54).*

Joseph is summoned to give his intepretation, which is "Behold, there come seven years of great plenty throughout all the land of Egypt, and there shall arise after them seven years of famine." As a consequence, Pharaoh puts Joseph in charge of stockpiling corn, and Egypt survives the years of famine. (*Genesis 41:1–32.*)

The Bible also contains dreams that teach and instruct. God shows Peter a vision of a large vessel, like "a great sheet knit at the four corners...wherein were all manner of four-footed beasts of the earth, and wild beasts, and creeping things, and fowls of the air." Although a voice tells Peter to kill and eat, he refuses, and says, "I have never eaten anything that is common or unclean." The voice tells him, "What God hath cleansed, that call not thou common." (*Acts 10:10–17.*) This dream is to instruct Peter that he must preach to the Gentiles as well as to the Jews.

VISIONS & VISIONARIES

MANY PEOPLE HAVE CLAIMED TO HAVE HAD VISIONS,
AND USUALLY THESE VISIONS ARE OF A RELIGIOUS
NATURE. ALTHOUGH THE FANTASTIC AND SURREAL
OFTEN APPEAR IN OUR DREAMS, IF WE SEE THEM IN OUR
WAKING LIFE WE TEND TO DOUBT OUR STATE OF MIND.

From the age of 13, the French peasant Joan of Arc saw visions of saints. She also heard voices telling her to go and serve the Dauphin, and expel the English from France. Joan of Arc convinced the Dauphin of her divine mission, and dressed in white armor, led her troops in capturing Orléans. Charles VII was then crowned King of France in 1429. Joan of Arc was burned at the stake in Rouen in 1431 as a heretic, but was canonized in 1920.

Most religious visions are of the Blessed Virgin Mary. The best-known religious visions were to the 14-year-old Bernadette Soubrious at Lourdes

LOVE FEVER
On the ninth day of a feverish illness, the Italian poet Dante Alighieri (1265–1321) dreamt of angels leading him to his dead beloved, Beatrice. This painting, Dante's Dream, *is by Joseph Noel-Paton (1821–1901).*

A SAINTLY SLEEP
Joan of Arc Asleep *was painted by George William Joy*
(1844–1925). Joan of Arc claimed to see visions of saints
and to hear voices summoning her to a divine mission. The
success of this mission changed the course of French history.

in 1858, and to three children near Fatima in Portugal in 1917. At the last two sightings at Fatima, some 30,000 and 70,000 people saw a strange, moving light in the sky. Whether this was a vision or wish fulfillment can never be proved.

～◎～

A vision can often have lasting and powerful consequences. In 1823, Joseph Smith, a 17-year-old American farmhand, had a vision of an angel called Moroni, who told him that a set of gold plates was buried in a nearby hillside. Miraculously, Joseph Smith found and dug up these plates. He translated their inscriptions with divine assistance, and the resulting Mormon church has over six million members worldwide.

～◎～

Visions are not always religious, however, and many people have claimed to receive visitations from the spirits of close friends or relatives at the exact moment of their death.

SIGMUND FREUD

DREAM ANALYSIS WAS MADE INTELLECTUALLY
ACCEPTABLE BY FREUD, IF NOT ENTIRELY
RESPECTABLE. HE TAUGHT THAT DREAM SYMBOLS
DISGUISE UNPALATABLE TRUTHS, BUT HIS APPROACH
TO INTERPRETING DREAMS HAS MANY DETRACTORS.

After training in neurology, Sigmund Freud (1856–1939) began to practice what later became psychoanalysis. Initially, following his colleague Josef Breuer (1842–1925), he used hypnosis to treat cases of hysteria. He then replaced hypnosis with the technique of free association and began to explore his patients' dreams for clues to their problems.

Freud believed that dreams were wish fulfillment – in our dreams we represent our deepest desires, which in an adult are nearly always sexual. However, because these desires would be offensive to our sleeping conscious minds, our censor, or superego, disguises our true intentions. The obscurity of dreams, Freud

SUPEREGO CENSOR
Sigmund Freud codified and popularized several existing ideas of dream interpretation, but the theory of our superego censor repressing or disguising the desires of our subconscious mind appears to be original to him.

said, "is due to alterations in repressed material made by the censorship." However, this theory does not explain why we might have a heavily disguised dream one night and a straightforward dream of the same activity on another night.

~ ○ ~

There are many problems with Freud's ideas, but he must be given credit for being one of the first modern thinkers to reexamine the symbolism of dreams.

However, he must also be criticized for seeing nearly every dream symbol in purely sexual terms.

~ ○ ~

Freud's detractors also complain that his theories, based on evidence drawn from his psychologically disturbed patients, were not universally applicable. Despite these criticisms, Freud created psychoanalysis almost single-handedly, and built a solid base for dream analysts to expand.

DREAM COUCH
Freud's patients lay on this couch while relating their dreams to him. Freud sat behind them in order not to disturb their concentration.

CARL JUNG

AS MUCH A PHILOSOPHER AS A PSYCHOLOGIST,
CARL JUNG INCLUDED ANTHROPOLOGY, RELIGION, AND
MYTHOLOGY IN HIS STUDIES. HE PROPOSED THE IDEA
OF THE "COLLECTIVE UNCONSCIOUS," A DEEP WELL OF
IMAGES AND STORIES SHARED BY EVERYONE.

Carl Jung (1875–1961) began
as a follower of Freud's
theories, but broke away in
1913 to pursue his own path.
Jung believed that the content
of a dream was meaningful.
"Dreams may give expression
to ineluctable truths, to
philosophical pronouncements,
illusions, wild fantasies...
and heaven knows what
besides." His theory
of the "collective

**A CURIOUS
SUBJECT**
*Jung's curiosity
led him to study
many subjects.
Although best
known as a
psychologist, he
produced works
on symbolism,
alchemy, and
even flying
saucers.*

POWERFUL
ARCHETYPES
*These Tarot cards –
the Fool and the
Wise Old Man – are
from* El Gran Tarot
Esoterico. *They
represent powerful
archetypes. Sometimes
archetypal figures might
appear in your dreams
as your anima or your
animus. The Wise Old
Man may symbolize a
male authority figure,
and the Fool might
symbolize you.*

unconscious" stated that
although the symbolism of
our dreams is personal, it
is often grounded in the
universal. After exploring the
religions and folklore of other
cultures, Jung discovered that
they shared many symbols,
and that these universal
symbols frequently occur in
our dreams. It is as if we all
use the same building blocks
in the creation of our dreams.

Jung also believed in the
persona – the image of our
personality that we project

onto the outside world – and
in the shadow – those parts
of our personality that are
kept hidden. It is the shadow
that can surface in our
dreams, often as other
characters who might be
aspects of ourselves. Related
to this belief is his concept of
the anima and the animus.
Sometimes our anima or
animus appears in our
dreams as a powerful
archetype, whose purpose
is to teach us what our
conscious, waking self refuses
to recognize or acknowledge.

CREATIVE
DREAMING

MANY ARTISTS AND SCIENTISTS HAVE FOUND
INSPIRATION FOR THEIR WORK IN DREAMS. THE
UNCONSCIOUS MIND CAN BRING FORTH IDEAS THAT
THE CONSCIOUS MIND MIGHT REJECT AS TOO BIZARRE.

For centuries, creative artists have used the ideas that have come from their dreams to fuel their work. One afternoon, the poet Samuel Taylor Coleridge (1772–1834) fell asleep while thinking about the court of Kubla Khan. When he woke from his dream, he found he had two or three hundred lines of a poem in his head, and started to write them down. After only 54 lines he was interrupted by "a person on business from Porlock," and by the time he returned to his desk, the rest of the poem *Kubla Khan* had vanished from his mind.

HYDE AND SEEK
Night after night, Robert Louis Stevenson (1850–94) returned to the next episode of the same dream. He dreamed of Mr. Hyde taking a powder and metamorphosing into Dr. Jekyll. This still from the 1931 film, Dr. Jekyll and Mr. Hyde, *shows Mr. Hyde preparing his transforming medicine.*

Im 1525 Jar nach dem pfingstag zwischen dem mitwoch und pfintztag In der nacht Im schlaff hab Ich dis gesicht gesehen wy vil grosser wasser vom himel fielen vnd das erst traff das ertrich bey 4 mill von mir mit einer solchen grawsamkeitt mit eynem ubergrossen rauschen vnd zersprützen vnd ertrenckt das gantz lant In solchem schrecken bin Ich erwacht ee dan dye andern wasser fielen vnd dye wasser dye do fielen dye waren fast gros vnd der fiel ettliche weitt ettliche neher vnd sy kamen so hoch herab das sy Im gedancken gleich langsam fielen aber do das erst wasser das das ertrich traff schier bey kam do fiel es mit einer solchen geschwindigkeytt wint vnd brausen vnd Ich so ser erschrack do Ich erwacht das mir mein gantzer leichnam zittert vnd lang nit recht zu mir selbs kam Aber do Ich am morgen auff stundt molt Ich hie oben wie Ichs gesehen hett Got wende alle ding zum besten

Albrecht Dürer

After discussing supernatural stories with Percy Bysshe Shelley, Lord Byron, and Byron's doctor, Mary Shelley (1797–1851) went to bed and had a powerful dream. The following day she began writing *Frankenstein; or The Modern Prometheus*, based on the previous night's dream.

Scientists have also been inspired by their dreams. The German chemist Friedrich Kekulé (1829–96) visualized the molecular structure of benzene as a carbon ring after dreaming of a row of carbon and hydrogen atoms closing in a ring, like a snake swallowing its tail.

LUCID
DREAMING

THIS CONSISTS OF TWO STRANDS – KNOWING IN YOUR DREAM THAT YOU ARE DREAMING, AND BEING ABLE TO AFFECT THE COURSE OF YOUR DREAM. A LUCID DREAMER SETS OUT TO DO THIS DELIBERATELY.

Although it may seem unlikely, it is possible to control your dreams. First, you should decide where you want your dream to take place. Next, you should decide on an awareness signal – something to remind your dreaming self that this is a dream. A common signal is to look at your hand in the dream. Having previously agreed with yourself that this should be the signal, when you find yourself looking at your hand it is likely that you will realize you are dreaming.

As you fall asleep, try to picture the place in your mind as clearly as possible.

DREAM CONTROL
Your mind is a storehouse of images and imaginary events. If you can decide what to think about when you are awake, it would seem logical for you to have the same control when you are asleep.

If you "arrive" there in your dream, then you have already exerted some control over the dream. Looking at your hand, you should then remember that this is a dream and not reality. In your dream, turn your hand

around and examine it. This is a conscious act, and if you can do this, you might be able to choose where to go, who to meet, and what to do and say in your dream.

Experienced lucid dreamers might agree beforehand with others that they will meet in a certain place, and in their dreams they meet and talk. Some claim that when they compare notes the next day, they all dreamed of the same place, the same people, and the same conversation.

UNCONSCIOUS ART
The Spanish surrealist Salvador Dali (1904–89) claimed that his work could only be appreciated by the unconscious. He used photographic clarity to depict contorted landscapes and figures that seem both nightmarish and disconcertingly familiar.

21

PRECOGNITIVE
DREAMS

MANY PEOPLE BELIEVE IT IS POSSIBLE TO DREAM OF
THE FUTURE. PRECOGNITIVE DREAMS MAY WARN OF
EVENTS ABOUT TO HAPPEN, BUT SOME PEOPLE SIMPLY
DISMISS THESE DREAMS AS COINCIDENCE.

Dreaming of an old friend the night before they contact you is fairly common.

However, it is difficult to know if you foretold that they would contact you or they "picked up" your dream. The two events could have been connected or purely coincidental.

~ ❀ ~

Many people claim they dreamed that the United States President John F. Kennedy was shot before it happened,

DIVINE DREAMS
The philosopher St. Thomas Aquinas (1224–74) distinguished between divine revelations and "unlawful and superstitious" dreams. He wrote, "It is the experience of all men that a dream contains some indication of the future. Therefore it is vain to deny that dreams have efficacy in divination."

but unfortunately there is no evidence of anyone writing down their dream before the assassination occurred. Of the millions of dreams that Americans dreamed during the weeks before November 22, 1963, many will have featured an expensive car, hundreds will have featured the president, and some will undoubtedly have shown his violent death. How many of these were genuine precognitive dreams is impossible to know.

~ ⁀ ~

Many people dream of a disaster, such as a plane crash, and change a flight they have already booked to another date. If the disaster occurs, they naturally believe they were saved by their precognitive dream. But why only this one person should be saved by their dream is a common question, and it is probable that people often have these dreams and then in reality nothing happens.

~ ⁀ ~

Some people do have a good track record of seeing the future in their dreams and keep careful written notes.

A DEATH FORETOLD
Years after the event, a friend of Abraham Lincoln claimed that Lincoln dreamed he saw a body lying in state in the White House. In his dream, Lincoln asked who was dead. "The president, killed by an assassin," he was told.

If you have a particularly powerful or disturbing dream, write it down as soon as possible, date it, and give a sealed copy of it to someone else. Remember to do this before the dream comes true, not afterward.

INTERPRETING
DREAM SYMBOLISM

YOUR DREAMS GIVE YOU A GREAT DEAL OF
INFORMATION ABOUT YOURSELF. DREAMS TEND TO BE
METAPHORS, AND IT CAN BE VERY VALUABLE TO STUDY
WHAT THEY ARE SAYING ABOUT YOU.

Sometimes dreams are a rerun of your life, but they usually contain their own story, combined with vivid imagery. The second-century Roman soothsayer Artemidorus wrote that "dreams and visions are infused into men for their advantage and instruction," but also warned that "the same dream does not always have the same meaning in each case and for each person."

DREAM BOOKS
Lewis Carroll's "Alice" books have the fantastic creatures, strange events, bemusing conversations, and inverted logic that often occur in dreams. This illustration, Alice and the Red Queen, is by John Tenniel (1820–1914).

Sigmund Freud described a number of fairly clear sexual symbols that often occur in people's dreams, and Carl Jung showed that there are many dream symbols that seem to be common to all humankind. However, you should never assume that these universal symbols apply to your individual dreams. It is always important to work out your own personal symbolism.

~ 9 ~

Although dreams are mainly visual, they often base their images on word play, proverbs, common sayings, and metaphors. Naturally, these will all vary according to your native language.

~ 9 ~

It should also be remembered that the meanings of symbols can change, especially in the contemporary age of rapid visual communication. Any "general" symbolic meaning might alter because of a popular film, a television series, or the fame of an international icon. For example, the word

To dream of drowning, shows you will be raised by friends

HEAD FIRST
This card is from a pack of 38, produced in England in 1840. Each of the small, etched cards gives a humorous illustration and interpretation of a dream.

"madonna" can now just as easily refer to the Virgin Mary or to an American pop star. Also, the swastika was once considered to be a symbol of good fortune. Now the swastika usually means extreme right-wing politics and racial hatred.

WHAT YOUR DREAMS
CAN REVEAL

DREAMS CAN SHOW WHAT YOU WANT, AND PERHAPS
WHAT YOU NEED. SOMETIMES THEY POINT OUT
INSECURITIES, IMBALANCES, OR PROBLEMS IN YOUR
LIFE THAT NEED TO BE RESOLVED.

SIBILANT SYMBOL
Many snakes are poisonous,
but when twined around a
staff, a snake symbolizes
healing. They represent
wisdom as well as
temptation, partly
because of the Garden
of Eden story. They
can also represent
sexuality, and a snake
curled with its tail in its
mouth is a symbol of
eternity and
reincarnation.

Some dreams are wish fulfillment,
but you may also dream of
things that you do not want. What you
want and what you need are not always the
same. Your unconscious may be pointing
out something that you need to do, even if
it is not what you consciously want to do.
For example, in waking life you might be
pursuing a feud with someone, but your

dreams may tell you that cooperation and reconciliation will be more useful. Listen to your dreams, because they are often wiser than your waking mind.

~ 9 ~

Everyone has insecurities, and in waking life, it is natural to overcompensate or try to hide them. Your dreams, however, reveal your hidden insecurities as a matter of course. Do not dismiss Freudian symbolism altogether. Many dreams are about sex, which is at the root of numerous insecurities. For example, for a man, dreaming of a broken pencil or a demolished chimney could well be a reference to a fear of impotence.

~ 9 ~

Recurrent dreams tend to occur because of very deeply rooted fears and insecurities. If you have a recurring dream, examine it carefully each time. Work out what it is trying to tell you, whether it is getting

any better or worse, and what you can do in your waking life in response to this recurring dream.

~ 9 ~

When you wake from a dream, get into the habit of writing it down immediately. Write down your feelings and impressions, too, and note unusual colors, specific numbers, or any names. These are all important when interpreting your dreams.

FALLING DOWN

Dreaming of falling often reveals insecurity. It could also refer to falling in love or into temptation. In your dream, are you falling from grace, denoting a spiritual problem, or from a position of power? Try to remember where you are falling from, and where and how you land.

COLORS

A COLOR MIGHT PREDOMINATE IN A DREAM, OR A
SYMBOL COULD BE AN UNUSUAL COLOR – FOR
EXAMPLE, A DOG MAY BE PURPLE. THE SYMBOLISM OF
COLORS IS LINKED TO RELIGION AND CAN HAVE
DIFFERENT CULTURAL MEANINGS. HOWEVER, CERTAIN
COLORS TEND TO HAVE SPECIFIC MEANINGS.

GOLD
This masculine color
represents richness and
royalty, particularly kingship.
Gold is the brightness of the
sun, and represents the
majesty of God. It can also
mean wealth, money, and by
extension, greed.

SILVER
The symbol of purity and
chastity, silver is the color of
the Moon. It therefore
represents mystical and
feminine spirituality and
wisdom, and the qualities
of a queen. Silver may also
refer to money.

RED

The most sexual of the colors, red is hot, masculine, and aggressive. It can also mean stop, and represents blood, danger, and vibrant life. It is a royal color in a religious sense; Christ's blood, and a cardinal's robes, are red.

WHITE

In the East, white is the color of death. In the West, a bride wears white to symbolize virginity, and white represents cleanness, purity, virtue, and goodness.

PURPLE

In ancient Rome, "taking the purple" meant becoming a Roman senator, and purple was the imperial color. It is the color of royalty, ruling, and bishops' vestments.

ORANGE
This is a bright, lively color, denoting spirituality in some religions; for instance, Krishna followers wear saffron robes. Orange is also a color of health.

GREEN
This color means go, natural goodness, a fresh start, and growth. However, green can also symbolize poison, jealousy, and inexperience.

30

BLACK
In the West, black signifies death. It can also mean secrecy, fear, depression, emptiness, and the unconscious mind. It is the absence of all light, and therefore, the absence of God. An evil person's soul is said to be black.

BROWN

The color brown should always be put in its context; it can be the goodness and richness of soil, but also the murkiness of mud. Brown is associated with the sensation of touch, and with the material world.

YELLOW

This can be a symbol of health (the brightness of the sun), or ill health (illnesses such as jaundice). In many cultures, yellow is the color of cowardice.

BLUE

This is a feminine color. It is the color of the sky and heaven. It symbolizes spirituality, purity, fidelity, clarity of thought, and the cool clearness of intellect and intuition. Dark blue and blue-green suggest the sea, and therefore, emotions.

ARCHETYPES

THE PEOPLE IN YOUR DREAMS ARE SOMETIMES REAL
PEOPLE FROM YOUR WAKING LIFE, BUT OFTEN THEY
REPRESENT ASPECTS OF YOUR PERSONALITY OR
ARCHETYPAL FIGURES. TRY TO IDENTIFY THEM AND
LISTEN TO WHAT THEY SAY.

There are many archetypal figures, known by many names and categorized in

REFLECTIONS
A mirror implies self-examination, but what you see may be deceptive or distorted. The Mirror of Venus *(1898) was painted by Edward Burne-Jones (1833–98).*

different ways, according to whether they are being described by, for example, a Freudian or a Jungian. A person in a dream could be both a real person and an archetypal figure; for example, if you dream that a friend is a priest or the Pope,

the dream could be telling you to go to that friend for spiritual advice. Many of the archetypes represented in the Major Arcana of the Tarot can also appear in your dreams.

~ 9 ~

Everyone has "masculine" and "feminine" traits. The anima represents "feminine" qualities, such as intuition, in a man. The animus represents "masculine" qualities, such as aggression, in a woman. Any woman in a man's dream might be his anima, and any man in a woman's dream might be her animus.

~ 9 ~

The many archetypes include the Stranger or Shadow, Twins, Hero, Fool, and Wise Old Man or Woman. Their symbolic meanings can be found in the A to Z of Dream Symbols (see pages 42–59).

MERLIN THE MAGICIAN

Merlin is an archetypal Magician and Vivien is a Sorceress rather than a High Priestess, but the distinction between these two archetypes is often blurred. Such characters in dreams might suggest that you need to pay more attention to the mystical and esoteric rather than to the conventional and orthodox. However, archetypes may also have a flip side – for example, the Magician can also be the Trickster. The Beguiling of Merlin (1870–74) was painted by Edward Burne-Jones.

NUMBERS

DEPENDING ON THE CONTEXT, NUMBERS IN DREAMS
MIGHT REFER TO DATES, THE NUMBER OF A HOUSE, OR
TO FINANCIAL FIGURES. NUMBERS ALSO HAVE
SYMBOLIC MEANINGS THAT MAY BE KNOWN ONLY TO
YOUR UNCONSCIOUS MIND.

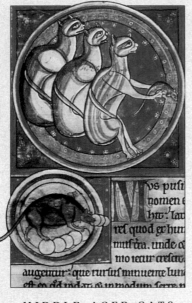

MIDDLE-AGED CATS
*These three cats holding a rat are
from a 13th-century bestiary,
which is a book containing
allegorical tales about animals.*

Symbolically, odd numbers are male, and even numbers are female. The meanings of the numbers zero to thirteen are:

ZERO: nothingness, a void, and emptiness;

ONE: man, loneliness, and ideas of unity and uniqueness;

TWO: woman, a pair, or an opposite, contrast, or choice;

THREE: the family, creation, and movement, each with a beginning, middle, and end;

FOUR: solidity, the gospels, seasons, compass points, elements, and functions of the mind – intellect, emotion, sensation, and intuition;

FIVE: the human (four limbs plus head), nature, life, the senses, and the occult;

SIX: sex – upward and downward triangles superimposed, and the Creation (six days);

SEVEN: heaven, a holy number, a day of rest, days of the week, notes of the scale, colors of the rainbow, pillars of wisdom, and wonders of the world;

EIGHT: infinity (when the number is turned on its side), material matters, worldly concerns, and the eightfold path of Buddhism;

LEONINE TIME

For centuries, people have been fascinated with the passage of the seasons and the numerical measurement of time. These images of the astrological sign Leo are from a French 15th-century Calendar and Book of Hours.

NINE: pregnancy, Buddhist spirituality, Chinese ultimate spiritual power, and great achievement;

TEN: the Commandments from the Old Testament, and according to Hinduism, the perfect number;

ELEVEN: revelation, intuition, self-knowledge, and a spiritual journey;

TWELVE: the passage of time, astrological signs of the zodiac, months of the year, and hours of the day;

THIRTEEN: often considered to be the unluckiest of all the numbers, particularly in the Western world.

ROOMS
IN A HOUSE

YOUR BODY IS THE HOME OF YOUR SPIRIT, AND IT HAS
LONG BEEN ACCEPTED THAT IN DREAMS, PARTS OF A
HOUSE MAY REPRESENT PARTS OF THE BODY AND THE
INNER PERSON WHO INHABITS THAT BODY.

According to the symbolism of dreams, everything in a house is part of you, whether physically, mentally, emotionally, or spiritually. As with all dream symbols, it is always important to interpret the meanings as they apply to you personally, and in the context of the dream.

ROOM WITH A VIEW
Windows represent your view of the world. If the curtains are drawn, perhaps you are shutting yourself in. Closed shutters suggest over-protection, and a smashed window could signify a fear of intrusion.

~~~

The facade of the house symbolizes the aspect of yourself that you present to the world. Walls represent security, or barriers against the outside world. If walls between rooms are too solid, it could mean that you are shutting off parts of yourself from each other. The porch is the place where you meet people and invite them into your life – therefore crossing the threshold is an important image. Open doors suggest an entrance to an aspect of yourself or, if the doors are closed, a barrier.

~~~

Inside the house, the attic or the top of the house is thought to symbolize the conscious mind and the intellect. An attic room sometimes contains many discarded but important objects from your life.

A HUMAN BUILDING
This engraving, from Tobias Cohn's Ma'aseh Tobiyyah *(Venice, 1721), compares a symbolic representation of a human body with the structure of a building. This is an ancient idea, which can be very illuminating in dream interpretation.*

The basement is the unconscious mind, and instinct. The bathroom represents cleansing, or purification, and the bedroom symbolizes rest, safety, and renewal. The kitchen suggests domesticity, warmth, and perhaps working in partnership. The living room is the heart and center of you. If someone else is in this room, establish whether they are welcome or if they are an intruder.

Balconies represent female breasts – a longing for the security of babyhood, or a sexual desire in an erotic dream. A hallway and corridors symbolize either the vagina (moving along them can represent sexual intercourse) or your passage along life's pathways. Stairs can also represent sexual intercourse, as well as your ascent to the higher aspects of life or your descent to the baser aspects.

ANIMALS

IN DREAMS, ANIMALS MAY APPEAR AS THEMSELVES OR
REPRESENT PEOPLE, OR PEOPLE MAY HAVE ANIMAL
CHARACTERISTICS. INTERPRETATION OF AN ANIMAL IN
A DREAM DEPENDS LARGELY ON YOUR PERSONAL
FEELINGS ABOUT THE ANIMAL.

Bees produce honey, which implies nourishment. They represent a group

PORKY PIG
A pig might suggest that you are greedy, but it could also refer to the nurturing warmth of the family.

working together and are a repository of wisdom; it is traditional to tell them news. Dreaming of a spider represents being trapped in its web or being devoured by a female.

~ 9 ~

Cats can be playful, but also willful. Catlike people might be elegant but cannot be trusted because of their

claws. The dog is a good companion. It can also be a hunter and guards the entrance to the Underworld.

~ 9 ~

Rats are intelligent and cunning, but are associated with disease. Mice are timid, and could mean that you are pointlessly running in a wheel or are caught in a trap.

~ 9 ~

Cows are placid, provide nourishment, and are a symbol of prosperity. Depending on the type, horses can be sturdy beasts of burden or fast-moving messengers. Horses can also symbolize controlled strength or a life that is galloping out of control. The lion is the king of the jungle, and symbolizes

A FROG'S KISS
If kissed, a frog might turn into a prince or princess. Are you hoping that someone will come along and transform your life?

If the goat butts you, your unconscious might be shaking your composure. Sheep suggest docile behavior, and may imply that you are too easily led. Rabbits can symbolize unchecked sexual behavior, but are also associated with gentleness. The monkey is a naughty, clever trickster, and could easily signify childish behavior.

watchfulness and strength. The wolf is a fierce, strong hunter, and is a metaphor for sexually predatory behavior. A goat symbolizes male sexuality.

THE WILY SNOOZE
A fox suggests that you should use animal cunning or that you feel hunted.

BIRDS

DREAMING OF BIRDS SYMBOLIZES THE DESIRE FOR
FREEDOM, THE FLIGHT OF THE IMAGINATION, AND THE
ASCENT TO HIGHER SPIRITUAL TRUTHS. FLOCKS OF
BIRDS CAN SUGGEST BEING, OR WANTING TO BE,
A MEMBER OF A GROUP.

Many individual birds have their own specific meanings, but remember, as always, to interpret birds in the personal context of your life as well as in the context of your dream.

A bird with a broken wing might show that you feel your hopes have been dashed. The albatross is a weight around your neck, but also the strength to make an arduous journey. A caged bird is beautiful but trapped; perhaps there is an aspect of yourself that you tend with care, but which is static in reality. The cockerel is a sexual reference; loud and proud, it might suggest there is something you wish to announce to the world. A crow is a scavenger, and symbolizes death, and the

FREEDOM FLIGHT
*Birds in dreams often represent the
desire for escape and the ability to
soar away from the daily problems
of life. This engraving from a
medieval manuscript shows some of
the birds that have individual,
specific symbolic meanings.*

dove is a universal symbol of peace, hope, and faithful love – the Holy Spirit in Christianity. The eagle represents noble strength and power, but it is also the greatest bird of prey, and perhaps you should beware of a predatory nature in yourself or other people. The hen represents fussiness and a lack of intelligence – perhaps you are being unnecessarily overprotective. A peacock signifies immortality, but its beauty contains a certain flashiness; therefore examine

yourself for vanity. The phoenix rising from the ashes represents a new start in life, and the pigeon is a messenger. Ravens suggest death, foreboding and prophecy – if they can be trusted. The seagull is associated with the sea, the ocean of your emotions. The vulture symbolizes death, but its function is to clear up the putrefying debris after death – perhaps this means that you have to clear out some of the dead areas in your life.

A WISE OLD BIRD
An owl is traditionally associated with wisdom. However, it can also represent cunning, duplicity, and death.

A TO Z
of DREAM SYMBOLS

THE FOLLOWING PAGES GIVE TRADITIONAL
INTERPRETATIONS OF THE MOST COMMON DREAM
SYMBOLS, BUT IT IS ALWAYS MOST IMPORTANT TO
WORK OUT YOUR OWN PERSONAL SYMBOLISM.

ACCIDENT This could be a premonition of a real accident, but it is more likely to be your subconscious mind worrying that your life is crashing. Your subconscious also may be suggesting that you deserve some form of punishment.

ACTING Do you feel that your life is an act or that someone else is directing it? Stage fright might mean nervousness about your real-life capabilities, and forgetting your lines suggests insecurity. If you are watching a play that represents your life, what lessons can you learn?

AIRPLANE Flying above problems, towards a goal, or flights of fancy, but with the implication that you are putting your trust in someone else (the pilot) to keep you safe. If you are the pilot, are you in full control? (See also *Flying*.)

ALCOHOL Relaxing your inhibitions. Do you need to unwind more? Or is it a warning to drink less? (See also *Wine*.)

APPLE Love, knowledge, and temptation. Its shape might also represent the female breast. (See also *Fruit*.)

ARMOR Protection. If it is too heavy, you may be erecting unnecessary barriers. If it is rusty, your protection may be insufficient. (See also *Shield*.)

ASCENDING A positive symbol, such as climbing the career ladder. It also symbolizes sexual intercourse. (See also *Climbing*.)

AUTUMN Seasons symbolize your stage of life, and autumn represents maturity, as well as melancholy and fading hope.

BABY The desire to have a baby, or a fresh start. If you are the baby, it can symbolize that you are yearning for simplicity or seeking protection from helplessness. (See also *Pregnancy*.)

BATHING Cleansing yourself. Bathing in the sea is linked with your emotions. Nude bathing suggests letting others see you as you really are and has sexual connotations. (See also *Dirty, Swimming, Washing*.)

BIBLE OR HOLY BOOK This signifies a need for spiritual instruction. Perhaps you are looking for moral guidance or feel a sense of holiness.

BLINDNESS Feeling cut off from every aspect of the outside world, or perhaps you are being blind to an essential aspect of

your life. Blindness can also suggest eye problems, so check with an ophthalmologist.

BLOOD Your life force. In some religions it is sacred because it represents your spirit. Spilled blood could mean a sacrifice, and bleeding from a part of your body might be a health warning. (See also *Wine*.)

BOOK A wealth of knowledge, your life story, or an example for you to follow. What do you need to learn? Look at the title, and read the words on the page.

BOX In mythology, Pandora's box contained all the troubles of the world, but also hope. Does your box contain memories, or aspects of your life that you have shut away? A box can also represent a coffin and death, or the womb and security.

BREASTS Caring, comfort, and nurturing motherhood, unless the dream is clearly sexual.

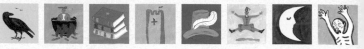

BRIDGE What is on the other side of the bridge? Should you cross over? If the bridge is broken, it suggests a breakdown in communication.

BURIED ALIVE A desire for a return to the safe darkness of the womb. If it is linked with physical breathlessness and a sense of fear, it could indicate a feeling of being trapped in your life, a genuine health problem, or simply bedding that is too heavy.

BUTTERFLY Fragile, perishable beauty. Also a warning of fickleness, or perhaps a deep yearning to be free from any restrictions. Emerging from a cocoon is a clear symbol of the transition to a new stage of life.

CASTLE An impregnable stronghold. Are you being besieged, or have you shut yourself off? Besieging a castle might represent an attempt at sexual conquest.

CASTRATION A fear of losing manhood and potency. It can also represent the struggle between the male and female aspects of a man's personality.

CEMETERY A place of death, but also peace. Perhaps you want to escape from, or bury, a problem in your life.

CHURCH The house of God. Are you in church to receive a message? A church also represents sanctuary. What are you fleeing from?

CIRCLE The circle of life, the seasons, rebirth, or immortality. Although the circle signifies wholeness and completion, it could also indicate that you are going around in circles. (See also *Wheel*.)

CLIMBING Pay attention to what you are climbing. If it is a rocky cliff, for example, it might indicate the difficulty of your ascent. (See also *Ascending*.)

44

CLOCK OR WATCH Perhaps a preoccupation with the passage of time, or the minutiae of life. Clockwork can refer to the heart's emotions and health.

CLOTHES How you present yourself. Wearing someone else's clothes can mean that you are taking on their role in life. Undressing suggests shedding your facade and has sexual connotations. (See also *Hat*.)

COLD Possibly a symbol of sexual frigidity; you are shut off from the warmth of the sun.

COOKING Preparing food means you are considering your physical and emotional nourishment as well as your health. Look at the ingredients for further clues. (See also *Eating, Hunger, Meal*.)

CORRIDOR, HALLWAY, OR PASSAGE Sexually, these areas represent the vagina; therefore moving along them symbolizes intercourse. They can also represent your journey towards a goal, or the passage of your life. What are you moving from, and to? (See also *Tunnel*.)

CROSSROADS A decision. Which way should you turn? If the "correct" direction is obvious in your dream, your unconscious may be telling your undecided conscious mind the right path to take. Take note of where the other roads go, even if you do not take them. If there is a signpost, try to read it. (See also *Road*.)

CROWN Royalty, grandeur, achievement, and the pinnacle of success. But a crown also means ultimate responsibility. If you put on a crown and it does not fit, you may be over-reaching yourself.

CUP Female sexuality. A cup, chalice, bowl, or dish can also represent the well of emotions. What does it contain? Is it full,

45

empty, or has it been spilled? It could indicate a spiritual goal. (See also *Glass of Water, Water.*)

DANCING A symbol of lovemaking. A ritual dance suggests a religious aspect; a frenetic dance could be the Dance of Death.

DAWN This represents hope, and the new – a new beginning, a new day, or a fresh start.

46

DAY A dream taking place in daytime refers to the conscious mind and the "everyday."

DEATH A new phase. A part of you needs to "die" in order to be reborn. Dreaming of someone else's death might reveal your hostility to that person, or it could represent a facet of your personality that needs to be disposed of. (See also *Killing.*)

DESCENDING Delving into the depths of your unconscious to seek something of value.

DEVIL A personification of a desire, drive, or ambition that your unconscious mind knows is wrong. The devil might also be someone immensely attractive who is leading you astray.

DIRTY Your unconscious is pointing out aspects of your life that need to be cleansed. Do you feel guilty? (See also *Bathing, Swimming, Washing.*)

DROWNING You are getting confused by your emotions; perhaps you feel you are drowning in your problems. (See also *Sea, Swimming.*)

EARTHQUAKE Possibly a vision of a real earthquake, or your unconscious warning you of an impending upheaval.

EATING Satisfying sexual and emotional as well as physical hunger. If you are being eaten, your unconscious is worried that you are being devoured. (See also *Cooking, Hunger, Meal.*)

EGG A symbol of new life and spiritual rebirth. If you are in the egg, a new phase of life lies ahead of you.

EYE The observer, who might be you, or someone who is watching you carefully. The eye, especially in the pyramid, is also an old symbol of the all-seeing power of God.

FAMILY A desire for security and belonging, especially if you dream of being a child. Individual members of your family are usually themselves or the roles they played in your life. Parents might appear in your dreams to express disapproval of your behavior even if you are an adult.

FIGHTING Usually a powerful internal struggle; the opponents are aspects of your personality at war with each other. Fighting could also refer to a conflict or battle in your waking life. (See also *Killing*.)

FILM OR POP STAR Hero worship or projection of an aspect of your personality onto the star. (See also *Hero, Star*.)

FIRE Seemingly contradictory meanings; fire can burn and destroy or cleanse and purify. It can refer to the fire of the passions, in which case it must be kept under control. It can also symbolize the Holy Spirit, or warmth and companionship.

FISH A symbol of the deep unconscious, creativity, Christianity, and the phallus.

FLOWER Beauty and the vitality of nature. Flowers also symbolize sexuality, usually female, depending on the shape of the flower. Opening buds suggest that you are about to blossom. (See also *Rose*.)

FLYING The yearning to soar in spiritual or intellectual ascent. It can also be a sign of escapism, but by looking down on your

47

life, you might be able to see new solutions to old problems. The feeling of flying in dreams can be intensely sensual. Who is flying with you? (See also *Airplane*; *Birds, pages 40–41*.)

FOG Doubt and uncertainty. You cannot see the path ahead clearly, your goals are hidden, or your emotions are confused.

FOOL This archetypal figure probably represents you stepping out naive and unprepared along a dangerous path. It implies that you need to take more care and consult your wiser aspects.

FOUNTAIN Water denotes the emotional and spiritual, and the energy of the fountain suggests the fountain of life, youth, and the fount of all wisdom. A powerfully spurting fountain might symbolize male sexuality.

FRUIT A symbol of a result or natural outcome, such as "being fruitful." (See also *Apple*.)

GAME Playing games can indicate that you take life too seriously, or they might mirror competitive situations. Athletic games may be a sexual symbol.

GARDEN Your inner life. If it is so tidy that it seems sterile, perhaps your life is too ordered. If it is overgrown, compare it with your waking life. If you can cultivate your garden, make it restful and colorful because this could transfer to your life. A garden can also have sexual connotations. Undergrowth, for example, can represent pubic hair, and a walled garden can signify sexual repression.

GHOST Do not be frightened of a ghost in your dream. It may be a "spiritual messenger" from a hidden part of yourself; therefore ask for its message.

GLASS OF WATER The need for spiritual sustenance, or it could simply mean that you are thirsty. (See also *Cup, Water*.)

GOD If you dream that God is speaking to you, listen very carefully. Whether it is God, your conscience, or your unconscious spirituality, the message will be significant.

HAIR Long, flowing hair expresses a desire for sensuality. An unwelcome haircut implies a fear of repression. Losing your hair suggests insecurity.

HANDS Are the hands moving in gestures of beckoning, applause, or warding off? Doing things with your hands might imply a practical application of your dream in your waking life.

HAT A statement about individuality or conformity, authority, the military, respect, or religious observance. (See also *Clothes*.)

HEAD The rational approach to a subject, and the dreamer's conscious mind. If the head is huge, perhaps you are arrogant.

HERO This archetypal figure is possibly a male or female warrior or perhaps a heroic film star. Courageous and strong, the hero could be showing a bold but difficult course that you should follow. (See also *Film or Pop Star*.)

HILL OR MOUNTAIN Gently rounded hills represent breasts, and climbing a hill could mean sexual activity. Climbing a mountain represents reaching toward a spiritual goal. Going rapidly downhill could mean that you are out of control in your life.

HEAT Sexual passion, but it could also mean that you are too hot-tempered. Extreme heat, as in waking life, suggests danger.

HUNGER Physical hunger; also symbolic of sexual desire and emotional hunger. It could also mean excessive hunger for power, prestige, or wealth. (See also *Cooking, Eating, Meal*.)

49

ICE Sexual frigidity. Melting ice might suggest that you are becoming a warmer person.

ILLNESS If you dream of a specific illness, it might be wise to consult a doctor. Illnesses sometimes have emotional causes. See if your dreams can help you to heal yourself.

INJURY Maybe you have been injured or are causing harm to others or to yourself.

INVISIBILITY Perhaps you are hiding, feel ashamed of something, or have a low self-image. Being invisible enables you to be a voyeur, but beware of seeing that which is better left unseen.

JOURNEY This could be a spiritual journey or voyage of discovery, perhaps self-discovery. It could also mean your daily journey through life, your life itself, or a real-life physical journey.

KEY According to Freud, a key and keyhole are sexual symbols. The key can also be the clue to a solution to a problem. In a dream of emotions, it could be the key to someone's heart.

KILLING If you kill someone from real life in your dream, perhaps this is a revelation of your unresolved anger toward that person. People in your dreams are often aspects of yourself. Is there a part of you that you hate or even that needs to be killed? (See also *Death, Fighting, Knife or Sword.*)

KISS Who are you kissing? Is the kiss purely wish fulfillment, the prelude to a longed-for sexual relationship? Or is it a social kiss, a kiss of allegiance to a monarch or a bishop, or a kiss of betrayal?

KNIFE OR SWORD According to Freud, a knife is a phallic symbol, and a sword is a penetrating erection. A knife or

sword can also mean cutting through problems sharply and incisively. A sword could represent the sword of justice or the sword of Damocles. (See also *Killing*.)

LADDER According to Freud, climbing a ladder means sexual intercourse (moving up and down). It could also refer to climbing the career or social ladder or to reaching greater heights in any endeavor.

LANGUAGE Being unable to understand the language you hear in your dream suggests a fear of insularity in your waking life. It can also imply a serious breakdown in verbal or other forms of communication.

LATE, BEING Insecurity and lack of self-confidence or an indication that you need to watch your punctuality more carefully. Also a yearning for more time and a wish that you were young again.

LIGHTNING Powerful natural forces or a thunderbolt from the god Thor with a message. A flash of illumination, revelation, and awareness that suddenly makes everything clear.

LOST, BEING An indication that you are going astray or are neglecting an important part of yourself. Also insecurity and lack of self-confidence. Who finds you, and who or what do they represent in your life?

LOVE Wish fulfillment. Who is the other person? Or possibly an expression of your desire or need for love. If it is family love, perhaps a wish for the security of childhood, or an indication that love is lacking in your current family.

MAP Reading a map suggests trying to find your way through life and planning its direction. If you have difficulty reading the map, perhaps you feel that you have lost your way in life.

MAZE OR LABYRINTH What are you searching for, at the center? What puzzle are you trying to solve?

MEAL Taking in physical and emotional nourishment. Also the companionship of people sharing a table, which can be spiritual or sexual. Who is with you and who is missing? (See also *Cooking*, *Eating*, *Hunger*.)

MILK A symbol of comfort and nourishment, especially mother's milk. It can also indicate a yearning for emotional support and has sexual connotations because of its color and consistency.

MONSTER A representation of your deeper, darker aspects, which in waking life are kept concealed. Try to learn about these aspects and integrate them safely within yourself. Monsters may also symbolize a major problem in your waking life. (See also *Nightmare*.)

MOON The Moon is symbolic of intuition, love and lunacy, poetry and deception, magic and mystery. It is the mystical side of religion, and in most cultures the Moon epitomizes the mysterious female – longed for, but the mistress of illusions.

MOUTH According to Freud, the mouth and all other orifices are equated with the vagina, but the mouth is also used for eating (physical and emotional sustenance), breathing (life and spiritual life), and communicating with others.

MUSIC Because music speaks to your deepest emotional roots, it can summon up many feelings. Is there harmony or disharmony? Are you creating the music or conducting it?

NAKEDNESS Perhaps you want other people to see you as you really are, or you may want to "bare your soul" or be the center of attention. If you feel

52

embarrassed, are you afraid of being uncovered in some way in your waking life? Nakedness could be a plea for a return to innocence, or brazen sexuality.

NIGHT Delving deeply into your unconscious, or perhaps there is much in your life that is hidden. Wandering in the dark could signify a lack of direction, and depression. Night is also the traditional time for romance and sex. Is it a sexual dream?

NIGHTMARE During a nightmare, keep calm, and try to step back, rather than be involved. What are you being shown? If you are still involved in the nightmare, approach the most terrifying part calmly and ask what it wants. Do not fear it, because it is probably part of yourself. (See also *Monster*.)

OLD AGE Time often swaps labels in dreams, and old age, late evening, autumn, or winter may all have the same meaning.

Old age might refer to your own old age or be suggesting that you compare yourself to your parents or grandparents and learn from any similarities. It could also be an archetype representing wisdom.

PEN OR PENCIL According to Freud, pens and pencils always represent the penis, and a dry pen or a broken pencil symbolizes impotence. But they are also used for writing. Is your unconscious sending you a message or suggesting that you communicate with someone?

PHOTOGRAPH OR PAINTING If a person is the subject of the photograph or painting, the person could be in the picture because you feel distant from them; possibly your normal image of the person is distanced from reality.

PILLAR OR COLUMN In Freudian symbolism, a penis. A broken column represents

53

impotence. Pillars or columns also represent strength and support. What or who are they supporting? Is it you?

PREGNANCY Sometimes a symbol is literal; perhaps you or your partner is pregnant or want to be. Also creativity and new beginnings. Metaphorically, are you "carrying" an idea, plan, or project that may be about to come to fruition? (See also *Baby*.)

PRIEST An authority figure, representing conventional attitudes to religious beliefs or morality, or a messenger from your unconscious. A priest might also represent important rites of passage, including christenings, funerals, and weddings. (See also *Wedding*.)

QUARREL Dreaming of a quarrel with someone implies there is something wrong with your real-life relationship even if it has not yet surfaced.

QUEEN OR KING Major archetypal figures or perhaps your mother or father. If you are the queen or king, is this by your own desire, indicating arrogance, or by public acclamation? It could symbolize authority, social status, or responsibility. Dreaming of the Queen of Heaven could represent the Virgin Mary.

RAIN Associated with the emotions. A light shower is refreshing, steady rain is depressing, and a heavy storm is oppressive and dangerous.

RAINBOW In religious symbolism, a sign of a covenant between God and mankind. Is there an equivalent in your life? In folklore, gold is at the end of the rainbow. Could this indicate that something beautiful will end in disappointment?

RIVER The river of life and the flow of the emotions. Is the water high or low, fast-flowing

54

or turgid? Where does the river come from and go to? If it is a canal rather than a river, maybe your emotions are too tightly channeled. (See also *Sea*.)

ROAD A portion of the path that you are following through life. Is it straight and clear or winding and interesting? Sidetracks might delay you, and a cul-de-sac is a dead end. Roadworks are obstacles between you and your goals. (See also *Crossroads*.)

ROPE If you are bound by ropes, remember that ultimately it is you who has tied them. Is there something in your waking life that will entangle you and restrict your choices?

ROSE Female sexuality and virginity (the rosebud), and the symbol of the Blessed Virgin Mary. In freemasonry, "under the rose" means a secret. The rose also signifies spiritual self-knowledge. (See also *Flower*.)

RUNNING According to Freud, sexual intercourse. But are you running away from something or someone? Or towards somewhere – a place of escape or safety? Is it a race? Do you long to be first, or do you fear that you are being left behind?

SCHOOL Revisiting old triumphs or torments; also, a need for a structured life. Who is teaching you, and what are you being taught? (See also *Teacher*.)

SEA The great sea of the emotions. Are you sailing calmly, or are you storm-tossed? If the sea seems threatening, perhaps you are fearful of deep emotions. The depths of the ocean represent your unconscious, and a long voyage can signify the voyage of your life. (See also *Drowning, River, Ship or Boat, Swimming*.)

SEARCHING What are you searching for? Is it happiness, security, friendship, love, a lost

55

part of yourself, the meaning to life, or anything else? Do you find it? Where?

SEX Possibly wish fulfillment. Who is the other person? If it is someone inappropriate, such as a married friend, the dream could be a safety valve for your feelings or a warning that you are getting too close. If it is a member of your family, try to analyze your emotional relationship. If your sexual orientation in the dream is different from waking life, the dream may be revealing an unacknowledged closeness with the other person, or perhaps you should pay more attention to your anima or animus.

SHIELD A shield is an essential part of armor. What are you protecting yourself from? What are you using? Are you hiding? Is the shield somebody you are sheltering behind? Or are you shielding someone else? (See also *Armor*.)

SHIP OR BOAT Venturing out on the sea of your emotions. Are you the captain or a passenger? Are you storm-tossed, calm, or stagnant? A ship's motion is sensual. Is this a sexual dream? (See also *Sea*.)

SILENCE AND DEAFNESS Is this an oppressive silence or a respite from the clatter of your life? If nobody can hear you speak, perhaps you feel ignored. If you are deaf to others, this could be a warning that you should listen more carefully.

SKY Spirituality, high ideals, or creative intellect. Is it peaceful or stormy? (See also *Airplane*; *Birds, pages 40–41, Flying, Lightning*.)

SPRING (SEASON) A fresh start, the promise of new life, childhood, and early youth.

SPRING (WATER) Fresh and life-giving, a source of healing and spirituality, and emotions.

56

STAR Hope and guidance. A five-pointed star may mean magic; a six-pointed star could refer to the Star of David, sexuality (see *Numbers, pages 34–35*), or the physical and the spiritual working together. A star might also refer to a starring role. (See also *Film or Pop Star.*)

STRANGER This archetypal figure is also known as the Shadow. It is probably half-hidden and unrecognized, and represents the darker, most negative, least pleasant, and most concealed aspects of your own personality.

SUMMER This season represents fulfillment, warmth, the goodness of nature, late youth, and early adulthood. In mythology, the Summer Land is known as a place of goodness.

SUN The giver of light, warmth, energy, and life. It might represent the glory of God, knowledge, and intellect, and

its light can reveal the truth. Although it is usually a positive symbol, it can also destroy.

SWIMMING According to Freud, swimming represents sexual intercourse. Water often symbolizes emotions, therefore swimming can mean being in control of your feelings. Are you keeping your head above water? Are you out of your depth or fighting against the tide? (See also *Bathing, Dirty, Drowning, Sea, Washing.*)

TEACHER An authority figure, expressing approval or disapproval. Perhaps the teacher is giving you an important lesson, in which case you should listen carefully. If you are the teacher, how is your class responding? (See also *School.*)

TOY A wish for childhood simplicity and security. What or whom does the toy represent? Perhaps you want to exert more control over certain elements of

your own life. Or does it signify your desire for control of real-life situations? Are you toying with someone or treating someone as a plaything?

TREE Stability and strength. Trees are alive, and might symbolize people. They can also be sacred; they join the ground (the material) to the sky (the spiritual). Many trees have spiritual significance, such as the World Tree (Yggdrasil) and the Tree of Life.

58

TUNNEL According to Freud, the vagina; therefore moving along it represents birth or sexual intercourse. Also the passage of life or a journey into your unconscious. What is at each end of the tunnel? (See also *Corridor, Hallway, or Passage.*)

TWINS Archetypal figures suggesting the need for balance, perhaps between your intellect and your intuition.

VALLEY A valley between gently folding hills (especially if there are scrubby bushes and a cleft, perhaps with a spring or stream) is a clear and common image of the female loins. Also the Valley of the Shadow of Death or the Vale of Sorrow.

WALL A barrier. Is it keeping you out, or shutting you in? Have you erected barriers between yourself and other people, or have you walled off parts of yourself?

WAR A battle, perhaps between your conscious and unconscious desires or your intellect and emotions. It could also be a metaphor for a conflict in your waking life.

WASHING What are you washing away? Are you abnegating responsibility or absolving yourself of guilt? Perhaps you need to examine your conscience. (See also *Bathing, Dirty, Swimming.*)

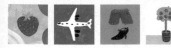

WATER Your emotions. Still waters represent the deep well of your emotions. Running water denotes lively emotions, and cleansing. Stagnant water suggests that your emotional life is unhealthy or dead. A dam indicates that you are bottling up your emotions. Also the water of life, as well as associations with spirituality, birth, and rebirth. (See also *Bathing, Glass of Water, River, Sea, Swimming.*)

WEDDING The formalization of an informal relationship; also a suggestion that two ideas should be brought together. It could also represent any other religious occasion. (See *Priest.*)

WHEEL The wheel of life. A wheel can represent a mandala, a mystical symbol of the pattern of life. The wheel can also symbolize the zodiacal circle or the wheel of fortune. If it is broken, it suggests your life has been derailed. (See also *Circle.*)

WIND Your spirit or the Holy Spirit. A breeze is refreshing; a hurricane is destructive.

WINE In the communion service, red wine and blood are interchangeable symbols, and red wine is a spiritual symbol for life. If your own wine is spilled, this could indicate self-sacrifice; if you spill someone else's, you might be spilling their blood. (See also *Alcohol, Blood.*)

WINTER Coldness, old age, and death, but probably emotional rather than physical death. The end of a natural cycle.

WISE OLD MAN OR WOMAN These archetypal figures sometimes appear as your father or mother, or as authority figures such as a king or queen, priest, teacher, or judge. The Wise Old Man or Woman is likely to be the voice of moral correctness, your unconscious, or perhaps your conscience telling you how to behave.

INDEX

ACKNOWLEDGMENTS

Artworks
Marion Deuchars 28, 29, 30, 31, 42, 43, 44, 45,
46, 47, 48, 49, 50, 51, 52, 53, 54, 55, 56, 57, 58, 59;
Anna Benjamin.

Special Photography
Steve Gorton and Sarah Ashun.
Thank you to the British Museum.

Additional Photography
Geoff Brightling, Jane Burton,
Karl Shone, Steve Shott, Kim Taylor.

Editorial assistance Martha Swift,
Picture research assistance Ingrid Nilsson,
DTP design assistance Daniel McCarthy.

Picture Credits

Key: *t* top; *c* center; *b* below; *l* left; *r* right

Bridgeman Art Library/Bury Art Gallery and Museum, *Dante's Dream from the
Divine Comedy*, Sir Joseph Noel-Paton 12*bl*, *front cover*/Christie's London,
Apples, Albert Moore 5*c*/*Giraudon*, *Joan of Arc Asleep*, George William Joy
13*t*/Giraudon/Musee des Beaux-Arts Rouen, *Joseph Explaining Pharoah's
Dreams*, Jean Adrien Guignet 11*tr*/Kunsthistorisches Museum Vienna, *A Vision*,
Albrecht Dürer 19*t*/Lady Lever Art Gallery, Port Sunlight, *The Beguiling of
Merlin*, Sir Edward Burne Jones 33*tr*/Museu Calouste Gulbenkian Lisbon,
The Mirror of Venus, Sir Edward Burne Jones 32*b*, *front cover*/Prado Madrid,
Solomon's Dream, Luca Giordano 10*c*/Private collection, *Bottom Asleep*,
Sir Hubert von Herkomer 4*c*, *front cover*/Whitford and Hughes London,
Scene from a Midsummer Night's Dream. Titania Arthur Wardle 9*t*, *front cover*;
ET Archive 34*l*, 35*b*; Mary Evans Picture Library 22*bl*, 24*bl*, *front cover*;
The Freud Museum 15*b*; Hulton-Deutsch Collection 20*r*; Images Colour
Library 8*r*, 37*tr*, 40*cr*; Range Pictures Ltd/The Bettman Archive 14*bl*, 16*bl*,
27*tr*/Springer 18*b*; Rex Features Ltd/Sipa Press 21*b*.